T0101786

WE GO ON

Kerry Hardie was born in 1951 and grew up in County Down. She now lives in County Kilkenny with her husband, the writer and artist Seán Hardie. Her poems have won many prizes, including the Michael Hartnett Award for Poetry, the National Poetry Prize (Ireland), the Katherine and Patrick Kavanagh Award, the James Joyce Suspended Sentence Award (Australia) and the Lawrence O'Shaughnessy Award for Poetry. Her poems have featured in The Penguin Book of Irish Poetry (2010) and *The Wake Forest Book of Irish Women's Poetry* (2011) as well as in ten Bloodaxe anthologies: *Staying Alive, Being Alive, Being Human, Essential Poems from the Staying Alive Trilogy, Staying Human, Soul Feast, In Person: World Poets, The Poetry Cure, The New Irish Poets* and *Modern Women Poets*.

She published six collections with Gallery Press: *A Furious Place* (1996), *Cry for the Hot Belly* (2000), *The Sky Didn't Fall* (2003), *The Silence Came Close* (2006), *Only This Room* (2009) and *The Ash and the Oak and the Wild Cherry Tree* (2012). Her *Selected Poems* (2011) was published by Gallery Press in Ireland and by Bloodaxe Books in Britain. Her seventh collection, *The Zebra Stood in the Night*, was published by Bloodaxe Books in 2014 and shortlisted for the *Irish Times*–Poetry Now Award, and followed by *Where Now Begins* (2020) and *We Go On* (2024).

Her first novel, *Hannie Bennet's Winter Marriage*, appeared in 2000; her second, *The Bird Woman*, was published in 2006. Kerry Hardie is a member of Aosdána.

KERRY HARDIE

We Go On

BLOODAXE BOOKS

ISBN: 978 1 78037 701 8

First published 2024 by
Bloodaxe Books Ltd,
Eastburn,
South Park,
Hexham,
Northumberland NE46 1BS.

www.bloodaxebooks.com
For further information about Bloodaxe titles
please visit our website and join our mailing list
or write to the above address for a catalogue.

Supported using public funding by
**ARTS COUNCIL
ENGLAND**

Cover design: Neil Astley & Pamela Robertson-Pearce

Printed in Great Britain by Bell & Bain Limited, Glasgow, Scotland, on
acid-free paper sourced from mills with FSC chain of custody certification.

For Seán,
and for my mother, Dorothy Jolley, 1921–2018

It is, in fact, the preparation for death, the ultimate
acceptance of it, that lends incomparable authority,
particularly in a culture like ours…where the
biggest taboo is our own mortality, not sex.
PAUL BAILEY, introduction to *Memoirs of Hadrian*
by Marguerite Yourcenar

He went in, not only through the worm-eaten
doorway of his worldly house, but on through
the secret inner door.
PATRICK WHITE, *Riders in the Chariot*

The sculptor of life is the threat of death.
ADAM NICOLSON

The touch of suffering is outrageous.
DAMIAN SMYTH, 'These Things', *Irish Street*

ACKNOWLEDGEMENTS

Acknowledgements are due to the following for first publication of some of these poems: *Archipelago, Days of Clear Light: A Festschrift in Honour of Jessie Lendennie and in Celebration of Salmon Press at 40* (Salmon Press, 2021), Poetry Ireland, *Stand, Well You Don't Look It* and *Write Where We Are Now* (ed. Carol Ann Duffy, Manchester Writing School, 2020).

Some poems also appeared in these publications by Kerry Hardie: *This Is the One Who Will Leave* (World Voices, http://chapbooks.webdelsol.com/worldvoices/index.htm), *A Lucky Woman*, the winning pamphlet in the 2021 iOTA SHOT Pamphlet Awards (Templar Poetry), and *Walls Are Made to Fall Down*, Clutag Poetry new series No.3 (Clutag Press, 2023).

Thanks to Moya Cannon for her unfailing friendship and advice, to Neil Astley for his care and dedication in putting this book together, to Dorothea Linder for her help and enthusiastic support, to Dr Val Lonergan for years of putting up with me as a patient, and to Amelia Stein for her beautiful photograph.

CONTENTS

Search

There is this secret running under life,
the thrust behind manifestation,
in how the form splits,
pushes up from the ground,
and the leaves grow and strengthen,
and the next branch begins its press
from the bark of the branch that came before,
and I'm looking everywhere for this secret,
always sorrowing,
one thing giving way to the next,
the secret still not revealed,

until at the year's end
when everything falls into winter again,
the secret grows stronger and stronger,
comes out of hiding,
becomes a great knowledge,
so powerful its presence here hurts –
and then the earth turns and the knowledge goes burrowing
down under manifestation all over again,
but visible, clearly laid out –
become birdsong like trickles of light,
become light running over still water.

Tangled

(i.m. my cousin, Rosaleen)

How can I begin to unwind you
from out of my life which had bobbined
a shared wooden reel since our childhood

shone the damp mornings, the waves
that licked at our feet, the milk
from the banded jug?

Both of us, trapped inside matter,
joyous and sorrowful, amazed
at all the long life stretched ahead –

Now matter has hardened to hardship, but still
I could not want you released
into the marvellous light.

Elsewhere

Fronded ash blows in the wind.
The young dog sleeps in the grass.
Bees pass.

A wash has been hung.

What is there,
now you have time?

Only love.
Washing.
Light through the trees and a blackbird's
chortled satisfaction.

You think you may be dissolving,
losing your definition.
For a minute or two you are wondering
why you are doing this nothing,
but then you float off into being.

It is hard coming back,
reclaiming your life in a body.
You feel a fretful discomfort.
Constricted, in a container.

It passes.
Already, you hardly remember.
You're sturdily inside the life
you think of as yours.

We Go On

There's a band of black weather under the rim of the sky,
then a shimmer of light, spreading the face of the sea.

A man walks a dog and gulls drape themselves
on the unseen flow of bright air –

and it feels like everything's happened already,
and everyone's fighting to board the last plane,

though the man is still walking the dog and more gulls
settle and stud the roof of an empty shed

and maybe it's always been this way,
with all of us sure of our own redemption:

though it's dark out there, we'll still muddle through,
and it's somebody else who'll fall off the edge of the world.

On Trauma, Sickness, Loss

Everyone who is alive and conscious moves constantly between their inwardness – the inner reality of our feelings, emotions, thoughts – and its opposite, the outer life of the 'real' physical world that is all around us. This subtle movement from inner to outer and back again is the stuff from which art is made.

But the process is never restricted to artists. Anyone who has lived through the death of someone they love will have experienced precisely this movement. In the process and aftermath of death it is almost as though the gates to our outer life are temporarily closed and the inner life overwhelms us. What was vital yesterday seems irrelevant today. Our outer life doesn't suddenly cease but we are forced more deeply into our inner life. It is like a sea mist descending. We can see the waves, advancing, withdrawing, lacing our feet, but the rest is lost in a grey blur, leached of colour and life. Yet our 'inwardness' becomes more intense. All our values are reversed.

The same thing happens when we are suddenly arrested in mid-stride by the onset of a life-threatening or incurable illness. Not only does our physical body have to cope with pain and intrusion, but all our convictions of 'who we are' become traumatised and distorted. Our bodies are threatened, so our inwardness moves centre stage.

Life – the whole of life – has to confront mortality and darkness as well as living and light. The Buddhists say that we can only truly live when we do not care whether we live or die. Acceptance of this reality lets us go beyond fear to dwell in some sort of serenity. Most of us can access this on an intellectual level but not when we are threatened with pain or even 'just' persistent discomfort. We scuttle back into our bodies and yo yo between fear of non-existence and the urge to be released from the existence that is causing us such anguish.

Thus are we forced to seek out a new equilibrium. But before achieving any sort of balance we are thrown into a cycle of action and reaction and we ricochet back and forth between elevation and despair. It is my experience that this ricochet is never entirely stilled because we are human; nonetheless a new programme slowly establishes itself on our inwardness, as we are forced to let go of certainty. Sickness – especially sickness that we may or may not recover from – means vulnerability, dependency and, overwhelmingly, fear. It means the loss of our cherished notions of 'usefulness', and the realisation that mortality is not an avoidable option. There is also the obscure shame that we've somehow got ourselves into this unpleasant and undignified state in the first place.

Once or twice in my life I have been there, inside the serenity. It wasn't a place that I reached through faith or inner discipline. More like falling through a hole in the air and entering a layer of being I'd always known existed, but not on a conscious level. Everything slowed and calmed. Sometimes there was simply emptiness but always there was love as well.

I write *was*, not *is*, because there's never any guarantee that such access will happen again. Nonetheless when it has happened once there's a memory you can return to, a hope that the hole may open again and, if it does, you may fall through for good. Maybe this is even what dying is. Falling through.

The Task

There's a rush of life in September.
I never understand it,
the wind, the emptying light,
everything hovering on the edge

of what should be the final ending. Instead
there's this vigour of change, excitement
of low-flying jackdaws, of high-flying crows,
wrens flickering the gravel after rain,
skies dizzy with swallows and martins feeding up.

I'm trying to find my way back
to who I was before the darkness,
but today, deadheading Shasta daisies, I suddenly saw
that there's no going back.

All the city gates stand open, undefended. The task
is to walk on into a night
that sometimes feels like morning.
There's the list laid on the table,
as when we're packing up to go away.

Grief

(for Gerald Butt)

What do you do when you wake to the news
that an old friend has died in the night?
A queer heavy stillness settles the air
though a wind is riffling the tallest trees
that stand in the field of yourself.

You wait.

The loss seeps like rain,
it enters the dead leaves, the crumble of earth,
the place you'd prepared,
or thought you'd prepared,
though you now understand

you hadn't.

At the Château de Lavigny, Switzerland

(i.m. Valentina Gherman-Tăzlăuanu)

She has changed and put on make-up.
The flowers on the marquetry table
wait, carefully quiet as her face.
She says she is the editor
of Moldova's premier literary journal.

The elegant Pole who shoots art films
– long, slow takes in Paris cafés –
turns like a lizard following a fly
to stare at this woman,
the dignity of her title.

He takes down an atlas,
flicks through the index,
lays the great book
on the tooled leather table,
mellow with banking and peace.

Her country lies open before us.
She leans in, explaining its story.
The Soviets have left.
The soil is exhausted.
Their coastline was gulped by Ukraine.

We stand there, bent to the page,
like the sunflowers we passed in the fields
that dipped their great heads to beg grace.
She shrugs, folds her arms in defiance,
refuses to shrink or back off.

None of us can find a thing to say.

Where Do We Live?

This dream is full of rain and children's voices,
of wisps of mist that wrap themselves
round bird-sounds and a puddled light
that moves across a lake –

The children part the branches of a beech:
its lacing nets, its pointed buds. They run. I wake
inside the dream. Yet know I should be seeing
the hotel bed-lamp's glow.

I follow after the damp, rainy children.
Then voices, daylight, traffic streaming
through thin glass.
The children have all vanished,

gone off behind the curtains of raw light.

Walls Are Meant to Fall Down

There was a place we went to once in Spain.
I would climb up to where some ancient, broken wall still stood
and sit, my back against its warmth, and read.

It's easier to read like this, under a broken wall.
A broken wall is a place of ruin, the small plants lodged in its cracks
grow peacefully there, allowing for sunlight and endings.

Even now, in December, many years later,
in a rainy country, altogether other,
I feel the benison of broken walls.

How Was It That You Stayed So Long?

The worn tatters of once-was-a-garden.
Trees, pressed dark against a house.

A woman, sick, lying on rags.
Sky falling in through the roof.

Now is the time
to be leaving this place,

walking away
from sky-holes, from ruin,

heavy-leafed woods
all fading to past.

Whose is the voice
speaking these words?

Yours is the voice. Why do you ask?
Who knows where another dwells?

Whose Is the Song?

Scraping up the autumn
on the tines of a wire rake,
the antique flare of leaves on tousled grass,

aware that there is witness
from the stretched hills and the sky,
the settling of small birds, the fade of light.

A watchful, taut encryption.
Secret, close.
A shiver in the wind that sounds like rain.

We Disassemble That First Home

(for my sister)

I empty the nest-box that came from her house.
Earwigs and woodlice scuttle, they slide
from the tangle of moss that once fledged us.

And I know there is nothing of yours that I want now
except what had been,
a long time ago,

in that lost garden where our mother held our being.

Anniversary

(for Carmel)

A dog barks.
Voices blow on the wind.

The tide slides out
peaceful and easy.

Someone is always arriving,
someone is going away.

For you,
she was going away.

It was yesterday,
twenty years gone.

Even in sunlight,
alone.

September Light

The trees are darkening, filling up with God.
The light shines through in little gaps and splashes.
The long grey heron sits upon the weir.
The dogs are in the ditches nosing pheasants.

The other lives I might have lived
meander off down other roads
whose path still shows against the dusk
creeping the gold-light glow that holds the hills.

The Coracle Called *Trust-Me*

(for Gisela, a Sufi)

Trust-Me is a frail little boat,
badly caulked and holed in its sides.

Trust-Me climbs up the ridge of a wave,
slides over, rests in the hollow place,

sets off up the next frothing wave
slithers into the hollow place.

And on. And on. And on.
Bailing is useless, rational folk

prefer insurance to a spinning boat.

Anxiety

You hear the wind coming.
It starts below in the birches,
flutters up through the saplings,
reaches the meadow, lies down to doze in the sun.

You wake in the night.
You know the unquiet
inside you spells trouble.
You sigh and turn over.

Another wind starts up,
gets as far as the boundary wall,
falls asleep in the grass.
The sky goes on gathering.

Against Darkness

The magpies rattle, the light sits
in the cupped faces of the Japanese anemones
that are white as the inside of an eggshell
and stand to the wind.

Low cloud spills over
the shadowy bulk of the mountain,
while the sky higher up
is infinite and radiant, ships moving over it.

What are these numbered days
that unravel, never explaining themselves,
as though nothing is happening,
no history moving
                 in cloud-ships across brightness?

Thirteen

The old is dying yet the new cannot be born; in this
interregnum a great variety of morbid symptoms appear.

ANTONIO GRAMSCI

They have been here before
so they know their way round.
Only the child is unaware.

She stands, wide-eyed and steadfast,
one foot in the cradle, the other
ankle deep in blood, in menstrual stew

awash with flowers and kittens
and the lies we all repeat,
her legs long through the damp grass after rain.

The Muse Is a Red Dog

> It is the artist's job to collect detritus and guide it back
> towards earth's atmosphere
>
> PAUL MULDOON

Census

They sit round the table,
filling the spaces arranged on the form
Red dog snuffles the rat-holes,
checks the set traps,

smells a small rat-thing,
its death throes down there in the hole.
He comes back, they're still at the census.
He stands and stares up at the moon.

A door is pushed open, light spills on the yard,
he melts himself, darkens to darkness.
A darkness that's not in the census.
Nor a red dog, a dead rat.

Signs and Portents

Red dog is sleeping
but inside his dream
he is watching them readying the horses,

flinging up saddle bags,
tightening girths,
those Horsemen, preparing to ride –

He whimpers and turns, without waking.
When he does, he is shaken, unquiet.
He knows well the census is useless.

Not that Sort of Dog

They say the skulls of horses,
embedded in the walls of Orange Halls,

will amplify a pin-drop.
Red dog is solitary, wary.

He watches for the horses
going home for evening stabling.

He likes their long straight tails,
the sway of rounded rumps,

the clop of hooves on cobbles,
how the pigeons call.

He fears the Horsemen.
Hates his litter-mate, Black Dog.

Red dog at the shopping village

It's tiring away from the forest,
The people – their excitement –
all around him.

The rows of things on shiny shelves
have labels showing
marked down prices.

The armaments are in demand.
They are efficient
and long-lasting.

Winter

A cross-hatch of muscle,
bone-smell of black branches.
Red dog knows only
the crash into water,
the clatter of duck rising up.
Red dog is home in the world.
The world is home in red dog.

Spring

Sometimes a dollop of blossom
slides from a thorn tree and lands
slop-slap in a puddle and floats,

and red dog whirls, giddy with joy,
he frolics about on the graves
because he is still alive-alive-oh

and May is as green as the grass
and the dead are there, all around him,
scampering about in the light.

Summer

Something about today doesn't work
and the greenwood has gone missing.

This happens.
Red dog will snuffle the fields,

He will drink from the ditches,
wait for the forest's return.

The forest. Its cool depths,
dappled paths, secret ways.

If the forest comes back,
he'll be waiting.

Autumn

Red dog sniffs at the grave-mounds,
raises his head

licks at the wind,
trots back into the greenwood.

Red dog is tired
he wants to lie down,

to flatten the dry grass
into a nest

wait for the terror
to pass.

Far off,
he still hears the Horsemen.

Breakdown

It was gentle enough at the start.
The garden tools being moved around,

the hens let out, bank cards secreted,
labels changed on jars.

Time passed, they learned each other's ways,
destruction grew more intimate, precise.

They knew they had to sit it out, pretend
that what was happening was normal.

As for the razor blades, embedded in the soap –
They cast each misdeed at the other's door.

And I'm wondering how it has come to this,

when it still feels as though we're just starting out, and sometime quite soon we may learn what it is we are meant to be doing. And his eyes are very tired and very innocent, a man who is simply worn out by it all, trusting us to be there, to say goodbye without saying goodbye, to sit for a while resting briefly inside his great frailty then reverse ourselves out of what's left of his life, life being that which we carry around with us, each of us living inside it, or maybe it living inside us, tied to the meat-and-bone part of ourselves, which is all that we are except for everything else – everything passionate and raw and belonging to us alone.

Achill Lines

(i.m. Joan Margarit)

On the table, the book of his dying,
his emptying himself of his epoch.

Enough, he is saying, enough.
Calm, he awaits his last absence.

Little beyond his own memories
awakens anguish or fear,

though his country's ruinous story
beats behind his eyes.

*

I lift my own eyes from the page
to washing, blown on the line,

the shadows it throws on the sheep-shorn grass
where starlings scurry and peck.

Shadows and sheep and words.
Shirts, with wind-billowed sleeves.

Speak to me Joan,
from wherever you've gone,

the dogs bay here, too,
and it's lonely.

The Courage Coin

She tells me how she fears darkness –
its damp hand pressed to her throat,
its smother and grope, forcing her back,
into the safety of light.

She has proved herself over and over.
I can't quite finger the reason
for this odd admission of weakness,
this assertive claiming of fear.

Then I see her glance at the daughter –
fourteen years old, brown hair, frayed jeans –
forming herself into Hero,
ready for taking the world.

The husband and brother, both watching,
knowing that something is happening,
some tune that is sung in a parallel world,
pitched too high for their hearing.

Then she plucks a coin from the darkness,
holds it out to the daughter.
Quit the hearth and the stove, child.
Now is the time to leave hold of your senses,

get out there. Cry to the moon.

Those 'Homes'

Things weren't the way they are now.
You were scouring pots, scrubbing sheets,
people shouted, no one worried much
if you were happy, they were too busy
keeping you clothed, fed, and more than likely
you were doing the same, helping to keep
the younger ones fed, that is.
                              Then one day
you found a place like a well
that was full up with water – such sweetness –
and it was inside you, you went there,
over and over, it never ran dry.
After a while
you stopped being frightened, stopped being careful,
you sang as you worked,
you went back and went back, even when you suspected.

Then everything was different because
there was something,
something alive
inside the well, you were frightened,
he was frightened,
he stopped coming back,
everyone was angry, they sent you off somewhere,
even if they loved you, they still sent you off.
You weren't surprised, it wasn't as though
you didn't know and it had never happened
to anyone else.
                        So there it was.
Such a brief flowering.
Too late for sorry now.

Just Another Bomb, Belfast 1974

(for my sister)

You see, I knew where it was you were going,
and who you were meeting.

When I heard the blast, muffled by closeness,
I knew.

I remember the   egg-timer stillness,
the mist of fine rain   adrift through the open skylight
falling out of the summer night and into the room.

I don't know how long I sat there   unable to rise from the chair,
to get down the stairs,   open the door,   walk the few streets.
Then the sirens, the shouting, the smoke.
I don't know how long.

But I did,
            it was all   just as expected –
The blown pub, the fire, the flakes of black ash,
the soldiers, the small crowd who'd gathered
and stood now   silently   watching.

I saw you then,
standing among them.
I did not call out   but walked up behind you.
You turned to me saying you'd gone in to find her,
but there was no sign, so you'd come out and waited.
Then there was the bomb.

I remember the soft rain   moisture   or tears,
some dampness spilled over, to run down my face.

Yesterday

we watched as your long wicker basket
was lowered

and someone spoke
and people threw flowers and lumps of red clay

down onto the lid
then the hole was filled in.

I want to write words
about spirits rising

but that was all said
in the church and besides

this earth-part seems realer although
I don't know

how many more
of these things I can stand –

it isn't even
the empty chair or the filled-in hole, it's

the sandwiches,
the chatter, chatter, chatter.

The New Dead

Our bodies come from the earth, belong to the earth,
yearn to lie down in the earth and rest, to look up

at the black light over the valley, everything staged
for a world we no longer inhabit.

Ours is the wonder of non-being, passing beyond –
our flesh of no more concern

than a daisy picked by a child and let fall,
or a rabbit, after the jacketing knife

has slid down its belly,
unpeeled the warm coat,

leaving entrails and bones
muddling the blood-grained deal table.

Herself

An old, barren ewe,
escaped up the mountain,
resentful, defiant,
alert for the round-up,
the tight-circling dogs,
the tup and the slaughter,

her yellow eyes, curling horns,
brittle-legged skitter,
she stands against shoals
of lozenged sea-glitter,
all shift and slide,
and gannets, stone-dropping.

Impasse

(i.m. Jean and Barrie)

She was angry.
He kept moving away from her anger.
Today it was down to the lough,
he thought he would take out the boat,
there might be comfort in it and he'd get to lift a rod,
though it was too bright, and they weren't rising.
He knew she was angry because
he was who he was, and he knew he was selfish and
he didn't want to lose her but this one
he had to stick on. Who else could he be
but himself? It seemed to have gone on like this
forever, even then.

The lough was splintered in light, the summer
had turned a brown heel, shaken her skirt, it was autumn,
the blue veils floated the land,
the low hills of Sligo
ran folded and pleated in distance.

She went to the gate and stood.
Then she walked back to the house, but didn't go in.
She knew she was right, her stubbornness finally
setting into courage. It wasn't easy
to stand ground and always in the past
she had let him advance towards her
and when she had seen the whites of his eyes
had walked forward, embraced him.
She had wanted not anger, but love. And neither was young.
So everything
was harder.

Now she passed petunias and nicotiana,
the purples and mauves he had tended.
This was the last of the colour.
And there was no comfort there either.
Lonely, lonely, lonely.
He at the lough's edge. She in the garden.

Trees in Late May

They've dressed themselves up
in all their new leaves

and are blowing about
in the dusk, in the wind,

translucent and wild,
revealing, concealing,

the hardened wood forming
beneath their soft darkness,

that fateful laying down
of the next ring.

Small Poem

Sometimes I feel myself
float free of questions,

I'm not clinging on,
am not in a hurry,

have let go the struggle
for balance, acceptance.

The outer life wanes,
the inner life waxes,

the circle is drawn –
water, on stone.

Cygnets

Such a twisting, a craning,
a writhing, a scratching,
a rolling and plunging
under brown waters.
Five of them,
grown, but still grey,
the white pushing through,
and you never saw itch like it.

Then suddenly still and adrift.
Blank, dazed, at rest on the river.
Now they're lifting off, wings stretched and furious,
beating down onto the water
like young ones with sex strong upon them,
and no way around
the vivid pain of it,
eating them up from inside.

Pain

On the wall of this room, a small print:
an old man sits on a rock,
that sits on the slope of a mountain.

His robes hang, indigo, tattered,
his black pigs mill at his feet,
his beard wisps in flittery grey.

The light of the years has him faded,
till he's sketchy as cirrus cloud stretched on a sky
that's blue as a winter Bellini.

Yet his pigs rootle, blacker and busier,
they grub through the flesh of my shoulder,
their hooves dig, cloven and sharp.

Shell People

It's the sand
under my feet,
the very fine, very white
sand

and the shells
in the dunes,
sea holly,
succulents,

it's this that makes me feel
weightless
and outside of time
because it is *always*,

always there, back in time,
not the childhood of buckets-and-spades,
but the childhood of back, back,
such a long, long way back,

when the bare-footed two-legs,
squatted – their calls,
small, anxious and shy
like lost birds.

Vikings

How they love the wicked side of winter.
The broken walls, the fox-torn ewe,
the drinking places stiffening into ice.
Gleeful, the rush to the killing,
the jeering jab and stab, the lust for plunder.

In the dusk of this winter morning,
the crows are flinging defiance.
Ragged and harsh, their dirty, black voices
complain the day that's breasting seas
of slate blue mountains, shifting cloudscapes, snow.

Black Radishes

(for Sonja Landweer)

We went there on her birthday. A white evening
early in springtime.
She was working in her garden
moving among the earthed-up rows
of dark green leafy plants she called black radishes;
beans, more advanced than anyone else's; tulips,
red with gold blazes, leaning to the sun.

'A garden is a lovesome thing.' I threw her the quote
as I stood on the path, filled with envy and happiness.
She smiled. It wasn't a real smile,
it was tired from sadness
and being misunderstood.

We followed her up the stairs; beads lay on the table.
Above it, in the roof-window, an emptiness of light.
She was used to it now, she said. This new window –
threading beads by daylight.
Wild cherry and ash
netted spaces of sky. Away off, a blue hill
peered over the river-plane.
Just the same you could tell
she had lost some safety.

She brought out cake and sat in a high-backed chair, talking
about war in Holland in her childhood. How her mother had
got flour, an egg or two. Some anniversary – everyone starving.

Her mother, breaking an egg
into the white bowl. The telephone ringing.
Lifting the receiver, hearing the message.
Putting down the receiver,
saying the words aloud.

Her mother understood them, and then she did.
Off in the dunes, they had just shot her father.

I asked if her mother had finished the cake. I suppose I wanted
to know if cake mattered even when they were shooting your
father, your husband. If you were hungry enough, that is. She
smiled, the same as before.

Then she started to tell us about when it ended.
She had told us before, I don't know why
she needed to tell it over again
slowly
on this still, pale evening.

The trainload of Dutch children sent to Switzerland for feeding.
The train travelling days, in fits and starts, through ruined
Germany. How it stopped one night at a platform in a camp.
And they were taken from it. And they lay in those wooden
bunks where Jews had lain.

The place was chock-a-block
with dead Jews.
Tier on tier
right to the ceiling.

I thought – it must be the garden.
The lovely quiet order of it.
Domestic, vulnerable.
I thought of our garden,
how it slopes to the whitethorns;
how it's there, reproachful,
to be attended, to be neglected,
mostly weedy, part overgrown,
like a scullery that will one day be ordered and therefore joyous
but, until then, goes on the way it is.

Her garden is not like that.
There, the songbird sings on the branch
of the tree where the hanged man swings.

So the words must be taken carefully, one by one,
from their flat dark box
with its fading indigo velvet.
One more time, and one more time.
The dead must be honoured.

I thought then of a time
when we will need to live less carelessly.
I'll sow black radishes
and care for them, so that they thrive.

The Departure

(for Fritz Rinagl)

First there were calls.
People phoning that she hadn't thought would phone.
It was confusing. See someone every day,
and they don't seem much different.

The hospital was a shock, the need for it.
She'd thought they could go on going on
more or less as they were,
day after day. Sort of for ever –

*

There were neighbours.
They watched with her, everyone watched.
It wasn't a question of love, it was the enmeshment.
All of their lives, how they lived,

inside the old coat – more patch than coat –
the pattern of ancient fields they all wore,
its dragged hem, stained sleeves, lining of moss.
The lost-ness. Inside the green spring.

*

He went. The branches tangled together.
The world closed quietly over.
The same, always the same.
We are. Then we are not.

World, World

(for Jessie Lendennie)

These days I pray to October, to light that is dying,
the last of it clinging
to leaves in the stillness.
Tomorrow the leaves may be gone.

I pray to the strumpet flare
of the wild cherry up on the hill,
I pray to the poplars,
their soft golden leaves.

I may be gone too, no one knows, no one knows.
The world is a song
that someone is singing,
but who sings the song?

Now the cherries are lain
on their rumpled bed,
the poplars have faded, the sun stretches out
on the old, heavy bones of the earth.

News from Ireland *1348*

The Black Death

...*'And because of fear and horror,*
men scarcely ventured to discharge works of piety and mercy,
namely visiting the sick and burying the dead...
the pestilence gathered strength in Kilkenny during Lent.
There was scarcely a house in which only one died
but commonly man and wife with their children all going one way,
namely crossing to death...'

'... *now I, Friar John Clyn,*
of the Order of Minors and convent of Kilkenny,
have written in this book these noteworthy events
that I know by faithful eye witness or by worthy reliable report.
And lest the writing should perish with the writer,
and the work fail together with the worker,
I am leaving parchment for the work to continue
if, by chance, in the future a man should remain surviving,
and anyone of the race of Adam should be able to escape this plague
and live to continue this work I have commenced.'

It is evening, it is springtime, in the week that follows Easter
and I listen in Kilkenny in the year of 2020,
and I hear them, from their plague pits
and their words are clear and simple,
do not speak to us of hardship,
lift your spirits to the spring.

Choosing Clothes for My Mother

3rd February 2018

I can't speak because
won't speak
am
too old
to learn
have seen
learned
not much
too much to be said

respecting

silence, suffering, decorum
not expecting
much out of life because of the sorrow,
all of the sorrow
the dead woman
is on the bed and it's too cold
for that blouse
find something
else

they turn off
the taped music when there's
no one here
no one's here
I am here

have to choose
clothes for the coffin, have to
keep her warm   never say
I can't, never

cry, not even this time
she wouldn't let us
and now
everyone
is dead or just
not here

Back Where We Began

(for Seán)

The world tilts
and the swallows flow
down its curved line to light.

Soon enough, December.
Gaunt trees, stark against the sky.
Running water, stilled.

Domestic War

After the bitter words – retreat, regroup.
He spades the thick soil of the lower beds,
I worry at deep-running roots of scutch
that tunnel through the irises, sweet williams, cranesbill
and choke the underbelly of the lady's mantle.

The garden is indifferent to our fighting.
We go in when the spring dusk fades the light,
I hold my hands under a jet of water,
scrub at dark stains in seams and folded places,
small soil-marked patches, obstinate as love.

John Anderson, My Jo

Today I lay,
my face pressed into

the warmth of your naked belly,
breathing your smell.

Outside was April.
Already the tulips,

gaudy, flamboyant, silks flaring,
were running the home stretch.

The Transparent Kaleidoscope

(for Sinéad Morrissey)

I opened your book and there was a poem,
my name in the dedication.

You wrote of a gift I had given you –
a mirrored kaleidoscope, clear,

fracturing whatever you aimed at
into a myriad versions with no colours to distract.

You were delighted. The glamour of ordinary
become a multiplicity of shape and light.

I remember it now, I found it in Italy,
along with a pair of fine leather gloves,

chrome yellow, beautiful, I never wore them,
had bought them only

because I wanted them badly.
That was years ago. I know now that you never saw me,

only reflecting versions
that flung themselves at you when we met,

pretending they were me.
Perhaps that always happens?

I fail all the time to peer down
into my cleft in the rock,

that shifting place where I live
and must, before long, leave behind

since the tide is flooding to full now,
drowning everything in limpid water

that is colourless but changes
all that seemed clear, revealed.

The Ground under My Feet

The morning light lies
on hummocky fields, early ploughing.
On the stretch of the slope
a new lamb rises, staggers.

I need to cross over into some place
where no one expects me to know what I'm doing,
some place where I'm not even trying
to understand or explain

why light matters,
and ploughing –
ordinary, earthy things,
the need to paint feet onto angels.

Witness

I am watching the garden, its grave beauty,
the narcissi, their frail green spears,
loitering the April dusk.

And jackdaws, standing on the empty chimney,
their bright intelligence, their blue-black gloss,
their bird-ness, their thick, throaty laughter.

Ah world, you don't know,
you don't care,
whether I love you or not.

A Fable

(for Michael Longley)

But the nightingale so loved the rose
that he wouldn't join the great flocking of birds,
who set off in search of the Source-of-All-Being,
but stayed to make songs to delight her.

For the face of the Simurg lies over the face of the waters
but the rose has only a sunny corner in someone's garden,
she blossoms and blows and her beauty fades,
while the nightingale sings and sings as her petals fall.

And what is the use of a high, cold, clearness,
and why must we journey so far, suffering ordeal,
to look on the face of what is Most Sacred,
when there's always a garden, always a rose?

'...but I'd rather you didn't tell anyone...'

Held secrets are those quiet dogs
you thought you'd trained and tamed,

but one clear night and off they go,
full-slaver with the pack,

to waste the lambs and bite the hand
that tries to hold them back.

Borders

...he was borne out under the fire of things,
days, words, visions, fusilades of poppies.

DAMIAN SMYTH

for we so love the world
we charge our only begotten

to fight and die
for all those portions of the earth

that we call ours,
oblivious of those other times

when someone else – not one of us –
believed it theirs

Empires

I woke early, turned on the radio for the news. It was
2003. In days the Americans would start bombing Iraq.
From the bookshelf in the library I took down a volume of
Miłosz, stood quietly turning its pages. Smells floated up,
and sounds. Europe, wooded and heavy with mud. I thought
of Darius, the Polish journalist I'd met in Switzerland,
only days before 9/11. Of the photos he'd shown. His
wife and infant daughter. I'd looked at the walls and
furnishings behind his wife's face, bent to their child.
Their apartment could have been anywhere in Eastern
Europe at that time. He'd said his father was a farmer
and for him the fall of Communism was very hard. For
himself, living and working in Warsaw, the future was
full of hope –

In New York we'd seen an exhibition on the Mongol
conquest. When the Mongols had enough land they
settled down, converted to Islam, began to crave beautiful
things for their horses and homes. We'd stood among
hangings of silk that had covered the walls of some long-
ago tent. Patterned lozenges gleamed from the borders:
hinds and fawns in bowery medallions, gold thread on green.
Their emperors had protected craftsmen, encouraged the
arts, sent their horsemen elsewhere, seeking out other
slaughters. A pleasure-dome was built in Xanadu. More
time passed and things fell apart. This is what happens.
Empires break up, new dynasties take over. Once again,
the refugees, the last planes leaving. The world goes on
turning. Sometimes the artefacts of tent or living-room
survive.

december's leavings

the air is still I stand outside
the late flowers burn
through the soft light

the bullfinches
in salmon coats
turn the spent leaves

toss sycamore floats
I watch their executioner's caps
the darkness deepens with each day

the slow curve
of a pheasant's head
stands proud against the yellowing grass

each day the fabric of the year
its sombre weave
shot through with grace –

In the End It Is a Very Private Struggle

(for Michael Casey)

How you must yearn to escape
the discipline of a sick body,

the feeding and cleaning and sprucing,
appointments, apologies, drugs,

the duty of always explaining,
pretending that all's almost fine.

Outside, the air flickers swallows.
Skies, wiped clean with September.

Body – listen – let go.

Collecting the Colony

That year was bent
under the weight of apples.
All the way back, the gold light,
the hive smell – honey and smoke –
the box of bees.

He'd asked how I would heft their weight
when I got home?
I'd said I had a wheelbarrow.
A wheelbarrow, a husband.
He said I was a lucky woman to have both.

Wasn't I just?
And the bright day,
the sticky print-marks on the wheel,
and something alive and tremendous
wedged in close behind the seat.

Post-war Story

We were children with pet rabbits. They were in a cage.
One night some Germans cut the wire and in the morning
the rabbits had gone. My mother told us they were hungry
– the Germans that is – and she made it sound quite
normal, and it was Germany so there were lots of Germans.
It was 1956, I was five years old. She said we must be
ready to get into the car, any time, day or night, because
the Russians had invaded Hungary and she might have to
drive across a border, but then the Russians shot some
leaders and went home.

I have never understood why anyone
would want to give children rabbits in cages.
The fetid smell of them, their quivering, frightened noses,
all the time waiting
for someone who's hungry.

Someone is always hungry.

Daughter of the House

(for my grandmother, Jessie Dale)

An old woman sits by a girl-child
holding a torch in her hand.
The pantry is unlit and cold,
the shelving is hewn from cut stone.

She lifts an egg from a galvanised pail,
turns it under the probe of the light,
seeking the fertilised blood-clot
that glows through the porcelain shell.

The child will carry the seal of this teaching,
stamped on the wax of her being.

That Box

(for Pat)

The morning is moody with rain and memory.
Spring blows in the wind, though the trees are unleafed.
I kept the key to your box in the drawer by the bed
but possessions, even your ashes, belong in the world and are
    worthless.

Re-shuffle the years. A child on a landing
against a black window, changed by the strangeness
of being only four years old and watching his first snow.
This picture, filed in my memory, I offer the world.

Nobody wants the picture, not even your sons.
Love is a blackbird that sings in a courtyard.
The courtyard falls into ruin.
The blackbird stands on a broken stone and sings.

Freshwater Swim

The heron flies silently
over the rush
and sigh of the weir,
the deeps of the river –

And here comes my body,
sliding along
with river rat, otter,
and paddle of mallard,

with meadowsweet, blowsily
sweeping the water,
with purple-spiked loosestrife
and fleshy agrimony

trailing the flow,
now new-sluiced with flood,
and emptying me
of all I call self,

dissolving it into
this long, ancient scoop,
where heron's stood fishing
since river was young.

When Oranges Were Spanish

Morning, in the winter classroom.
An orange – divided – handed round
and children spitting pips on wooden desks.

Not me, I swallow mine, the teacher
grabs my arm, shakes hard, she swears
they'll sprout inside me, I will be a tree –

I look. Already there is new bark on my wrists,
fresh twigs are bursting from my stiffening hands,
my flesh begins to flutter in a shift of leaves.

Oh joyousness, this stepping out
from my hot sausage-skin of human-ness
tight packed with organs, blood and veins.

Minute by minute I grow stronger, greener,
till I am tree and tree is me, and all the room
perfumed by orange blossom, Easter, far Seville,

till vision dims, becomes
reality of damp wool, chilblain-itch, yet still
the faintest tang of citrus hums the air.

Making Sense of Things

(for my sister-in-law, Jennifer)

And then one day
they decided to
he found out that
they got into a fight with
all the cattle died
they lost their jobs
she had twins

and everything

changed and the story began

to unwind and unravel
up hill and down dale
turning under-water somersaults
in seas red with blood
or floodlit by arc-light
or maybe by starlight
to the wailing of sirens
the babbling of geese

oh yes
oh no
no reason to stop
just to go on
and keep making stories
to tell to the children
the hungry
the hunted
the old and the haunted

to pass the time
mark the hour
find the answer
go on trying

Inviolate

The light of the hidden
is clear in the world,

everything stills
there is nothing to say,

nothing to love
except nothing itself,

vanishing into this absence
only the Presence is here.

NOTES

The Muse Is a Red Dog (29-32): a personal symbol of the creative unconscious, red dog crops up from time to time in my work and is the opposite of Black Dog, that well-known symbol of despair. The Four Horsemen are, of course, borrowed from the Bible.

Achill Lines (35): 'a book' refers to late poems of Joan Margarit, who died in 2021. Some of his work has been translated by Anna Crowe.

Those 'Homes' (37): the title refers to the Mother and Baby Homes, institutions run by the Church which operated throughout much of the 20th century in Ireland and mainly housed women who became pregnant outside marriage.

Just Another Bomb, Belfast 1974 (38): the sound of a bomb that is close is more muffled than that heard in distance.

News from Ireland, 1348 (55): the full text of the annals was originally translated by one Canon Carrigan in his *History of the Diocese of Ossory* and was later published by Four Courts Press, edited by Bernadette Williams (2007). The annals conclude with an entry written in a different hand, so presumably John Cline was also taken by the plague.

A Fable (65): *The Conference of the Birds* by Farid un-Din Attar, is the 12th-century story of the birds who travelled to find the Simurg, the Great Bird of Persian myth.

That Box (74): the last lines borrow an image from Joan Margarit's poem 'Works of love' about building a courtyard for a blackbird.